THE EVENT EFFECT

How to leverage event marketing to grow brands

3 22

THE EVENT EFFECT

How to leverage event marketing to grow brands

FIRST EDITION

DAVID MITROFF, PH.D.

A big thank you to those who have attended,
supported and sponsored our events.

To Moréa, friends, family and all of the employees,
interns and volunteers who have assisted us in
hosting, organizing and promoting premier and
memorable events over the last 15 years.

Thank you Albert, Alyson, Ana, Anand, Angel, Anne,
Antoine, Ari, Aylisha, Baba, Benny, Brenda, Brent,
Bri, Bruce, Caitlin, Cary, Chelsea, Clara, Cuong,
Dan, David, Deidre, Desiree, Don, Drew, Dylan,
Edward, Eric, Erik, Frederick, Galina, Gera, Greg,
Hannah, Henning, Issachar, Jackee, Jasmine, Jason,
Jeff, Joe, Jordan, Jossiel, Julie, Katy, Kaya, Kiana,
Kim, Lais, Layla, Lian, Livia, Mabel, Marc, Mark,
Markus, Matt, Melody, Michele, Michelle, Moshin,
Narumi, Neil, Nicole, Niven, Ola, Olivia, Pam,
Patrick, Paul, Pichaya, Poyi, Ricardo, Samantha,
Sophie, Steve, Susan, Tyler, Vera, and many more!

CONTENTS

ABOUT THE AUTHOR

David Mitroff, Ph.D. is a sought after business growth speaker, marketing expert and business consultant who shares creative ways for business professionals to digitally enhance their brand, generate business growth, and leverage their network.

With over a decade of experience, David has spoken at events all over the world including in Korea, China, and Turkey for organizations and companies including Google and AT&T and at conferences and association meetings for the Restaurant Executive Summit, Western Food Service Conference,

HardwareCon, the Association of Defense Counsel and many more.

David engages and motivates audiences by sharing his experiences from founding six companies - including a successful consulting firm, being a College Instructor in Marketing and Entrepreneurship at the University of California at Berkeley and mentoring founders of over 300+ startups as a Google Mentor and more.

Whether your event has 20 high level executives or 2000+ attendees, David excites and motivates them to take action.

David is also the Founder and Chief Consultant at Piedmont Avenue Consulting, Inc. (www.PiedmontAve.com), an Oakland, California based award winning business consulting and marketing firm with a proven track record of producing results.

David and his team advise clients on leveraging technology for creative initiatives from strategy through implementation. David's wealth of knowledge is transferred to clients, leading to increased sales, heightened customer experiences and enhanced relationship building techniques.

Dr. Mitroff has an extensive educational background, which includes a Doctorate in Clinical Psychology with coursework in Business Administration, Legal Studies, Marketing, Culinary

Arts and professional sales training. This provides a foundation for excellent critical and analytical thinking, business strategy, relationship building and networking.

He is a college instructor at the University of California, Berkeley in Marketing and Entrepreneurship for International Diploma Program and a Google Mentor for the Google Developers Launchpad Accelerator. David is also a Guest Lecturer at John F. Kennedy University, Diablo Valley College, City College of San Francisco and other colleges.

He has been featured as a business and media expert for NBC, ABC, Forbes, Entrepreneur, Inc., Washington Post, Chicago Tribune, The Meeting Professional, Hospitality Technology, California Lawyer and more.

Born in San Francisco and raised in the surrounding cities provides an in-depth personal knowledge of the entire SF Bay Area and a comprehensive network of contacts. To better serve his clients and the community David serves on numerous advisory boards. He enjoys traveling both Domestically (49/50 states) and Internationally (over 40 countries) to share his experiences and bring the world closer to Silicon Valley.

ABOUT PROFESSIONAL CONNECTOR EVENTS

Founded by David Mitroff, Ph.D., Professional Connector (www.ProfessionalConnector.com) hosts over 50 events each year for the last 8 years. We organize, promote, sponsor and/or are asked to speak at events. We currently run more than 25 successful San Francisco Bay Area networking and social media groups with a combined total membership of more than 100,000+ members. In addition, we have over 35,000+ email newsletter subscribers who have requested to receive our email newsletters. Most of our events are in the San Francisco Bay Area including monthly happy hours at the San Francisco W Hotel, Google San Francisco, General Assembly San Francisco and other venues. We have also produced and hosted events in Los Angeles, Beverly Hills, Orange County, Las Vegas, Nevada and Portland, Oregon.

Our business development, event planning and marketing services increase the organizations presence in the marketplace, create "front of mind" sales, enhance customer loyalty, and strengthen brand reputation. All our activities are designed to increase cash flow, secure the existing client base, and achieve higher profits and/or sales.

INTRODUCTION

There is no substitute for face-to-face meetings, conferences, workshops, trainings and events. Events can be stressful and overwhelming; however events create a great platform to promote your business, grow your network and boost employee and company morale.

Some benefits of having an event include:

- Reinforcement and enhancement of brand awareness - Throwing an event will help you get your company in the eye of more people.
- Lead generation - You are able to target people and follow up with them after the event.
- Creation of better relationships - Meet people who are interested in similar things as you and your business.

- Collaboration with others and development of partnerships
- Letting your audience know what's going on - Use Social Media to publicize and make it easy for your audience to find out what's going on with your business. It can also be a reminder to people that you exist.

If done correctly, event marketing can grow brands and can create what I call *The Event Effect* which occurs whether people attend the event or not. The idea is that people (customers, potential customers, strategic partners, potential strategic partners, etc.) like being invited to events instead of being sold to. Would you rather receive a cold call or email asking you to buy something or would you prefer being invited to an event? If someone continues to call and is trying to sell to you – you tell them to stop. If someone continues to email, trying to sell to you – you mark it as spam. Being invited to something makes you feel good about a brand, company, the person inviting you – whether you attend or not. If someone consistently calls or emails you over the course of a few months in a nice way to invite you to several events and you always say no – eventually you will have coffee or tea with them or give them some time on the phone or to meet in person to learn about what they do. In short, you feel you owe them something for all those invitations – This is what I call *The Event Effect*.

In this book, I will walk you through step-by-step how my team and I have organized, promoted, handled day of event issues and follow-up opportunities for over 1000+ successful events of all kinds from start to finish. This book focuses on smaller to medium sized events (20 to 500 people), although the techniques can be applied to larger conferences, festivals, and retreats to make them more effective as well. By following these techniques, you will be able to leverage event marketing to grow your brand, increase lead generation, and strengthen customer loyalty.

CHAPTER 1

BIGGEST FEAR: WHAT IF NO ONE COMES TO YOUR EVENT?!

I strongly believe that 80% of why you want to do an event is for creating brand awareness, product promotion, and as a general excuse to create a list of n e w contacts and reconnect with old contacts. These contacts can be cold called and emailed to sell (without selling) to get them to know who are and what you offer. When it comes to events there are two options:

The first is where you host an event that you actually want people to attend. You map it out, promote it, get people to attend and follow up with attendees. In this approach, you have to put in a fair amount of work to get people to come to the event, however it is real event. This is described in this book!

The second approach gives you almost the same benefits, without as much work. With this option, you do not actually have to throw an event. You will still list the event on all of your social media sites, websites and in your email newsletter. You will still invite people, but you do not have to worry about whether anyone shows up or not because the event is designed so the odds of people showing up are very low. I typically call these events Question and Answer (Q & A) events.

What are Question and Answer Events? You select a time of the day where you are already at your office or will be at a coffee shop or hotel lobby while you are traveling. Whatever time you decide, let people know when and where you will be to answer any questions they may have about your products or services and how your business works. For example, if you are a financial services firm, you can say, "Come by our office at 9am to meet with one of our financial experts" or "have any of your questions answered on Estate Planning for HealthCare Professionals" and anything else you offer–it's as simple as that. If someone wants to come in at that time to have their questions answered, while you are already at the office, then they can. This creates brand awareness and can lead to business growth.

Keep in mind that this is not a workshop or training. You do not provide bagels or coffee (unless your office already has it). In fact, you are not providing anything but answers to their questions - IF someone actually shows up and has questions. If no one shows up, that's also okay. The odds are that no one will show up; however, six months from now someone will do a Google search on that particular topic "Estate Planning for HealthCare Professionals" and they will find your event and call you.

The purpose of these Question and Answer Events is so that you will rank higher on search engines, social networks and more importantly stay relevant in people's minds. You can get most of the benefits of doing an event without all the work of actually conducting a big event. For these events you are still cold calling and emailing people to invite them to come. It allows you to engage in more ways than you previously had and without selling because you are inviting people to learn from you. Even if no one comes in, that's okay because it still serves the same purpose of around 80% of why most people produce events.

In this book we talk about producing real events, however many of the techniques outlined also work for the Question and Answer Events.

CHAPTER 2

GETTING STARTED: PRE-EVENT STRATEGIES

"Make every detail perfect, and limit the number of details to perfect." – Jack Dorsey, Co-Founder, CEO, Twitter

You have an event to organize, now what? I have hosted hundreds of events in the San Francisco Bay Area and beyond. Below I have created a list of actions for you to take in order to make your event a success.

Creating a Strategy: Before organizing and setting up the event, create a strategy that is clear and defined. Your strategy could include the following elements:

Where:

- Where will you hold the event? At a convention center,

hotel, company office, community center, local restaurant, or country club?

- Where will you promote the event (Online, Flyers, Partnerships, Community Calendars, Community Groups, Alumni Newsletter)?

When:

- What time of the year will the event be held?
- When will you time your announcements and invites?

What:

- What does success look like? How will you measure it?
- How long will the event be?

Who:

- How big will this event be?
- Who do you invite?
- How many people do you expect?

Budget:

- How much money will the event cost?
- What will be the cost for attending?
- What do you have available in your budget?
- How much will you need to spend on staffing resources?

Theme:

- What will the theme of your event be?
- Do you even need there to be a theme?
- Do you need live music, what kind of ambiance do you want to create, will there be food/drink sampling, etc.?
- Who will be the host or emcee?
- Co-produce the event with another company or association?
- Having a Keynote Speaker? Panel of experts?
- Securing event sponsors?
- Will you partner with media, associations, etc.?

Keep in mind that securing a space is the most critical and hardest part! Choosing the right venue can be a difficult task. Before you start looking, determine the number of ideal attendees for your event. Keep in mind factors like whether it will be day or night, inside or outside, age range of guests, food and accommodations, etc. How far in advance is best to book your venue? Typically, 90 days or more is a good time to lock in a venue so you can start planning the rest of the event. For big conferences and sales events this may be years in advance.

Tip: Start with a smaller venue and sell out. Also use sites like www.Peerspace.com or www.LiquidSpace.com to find venues.

CHAPTER 3

CREATE AN EVENT PAGE: WEBSITE & TICKET REGISTRATION

Create the Event Page Using Your Website:

The first option is to use your current website to create a webpage listing your event. Using your current website, you can create an "upcoming events" section to list your events on. If you do not have a website you want to use to host the event page, you can always create a new one using Wix or WordPress.

Create the Event Page using an Event Registration Site:

The second option is to use Eventbrite or another event registration platform (if you don't have a website, this is an easy way to set up your event page). Using such platforms make it easy to start selling tickets and promoting the event instantly.

Tip #1: Do not post more than two of the same event at once. For example: Posting six months of monthly happy hours will make people think they can skip this month or next and go four months from now. This makes your event feel less special. Remember to make it easy for people tell multiple events apart (if you have other events listed on your page).

Tip #2: Once your event page is published, if any major changes are made, they need to be announced through email.

Event pages allow you to get the word out about your business and because events are current they show up today in search engine results! Current events also show up higher in Social Media results because they are happening in the real world. These event pages can help you reach a larger audience and make your job a little bit easier.

Event Website:

- ☐ Use your current business website?
- ☐ Create a new website (Wordpress, Wix)
- ☐ Create an event registration page (Eventbrite)

Event Page needs to includes the following:

- ☐ Basic event details (event description, location, how to register, etc.)
- ☐ Integration of social media
- ☐ Focus on registrations
- ☐ Easy to tell multiple events apart (if you have other events listed on your page)

  Tip: do not post two of the same events at once.

To Charge or Not To Charge:

Charging increases the odds of people showing to an event because based on my experience people who pay $10 or more are 85% likely to show up. For free events you can expect 40% to 60% of people who registered to show up, which can increase or decrease based on the theme, location, day, weather, if someone famous will be there, etc. Keep in mind that also as the price goes higher, around $75 or more, companies are often paying rather than individuals and this often means the attendance rates go back down based on conflicting work issues.

Deciding to charge a fee or make the event free is based on many factors:

- Do you have costs to produce the event? What is the Return On your Investment (ROI) – will the event lead to business or donations?

- Are you inviting potential clients or partners? It is weird to charge people you are trying to get to become clients.

- Are you early on in producing events or hosting this event for the first time? To get experience and to get more people to attend you might want to charge less or no fees.

- Promoting your restaurant, store or location? You want to drive traffic to your business location – then why charge?

If you decide to charge a fee for attending the event, try to collect the payment online during the registration process. This minimizes the check-in process on the day of the event by cutting down on collecting money at the door.

Ticket Registration:

When setting up the ticket registration, be sure to collect the attendees' information; not just their name and email. You can decide how much information you want to collect from your attendees. Ideally, you want to collect attendee data that includes first name, last name, company, job tile, email, phone number, etc. at a minimum. Sometimes I also collect their mailing address or ask questions. Make sure a confirmation email goes out to each registrant as soon as possible. This ensures that the registration process is completed and that they have a receipt of the transaction.

When setting up the ticket registration form (on platforms such as Eventbrite), try not to ask too many questions. If the registration form is too complicated or time consuming, people won't want to go through the process of completing the registration.

If you are interested in collecting information on what is expected of the event, give registrants the option of completing a pre-event survey, asking what they want and expect from the event. This will help ensure you're providing value to your attendees. To reduce problems, refund issues, privacy concerns related to personal data, videos and photos disclosures, etc. it is highly recommended to include a "Terms and Conditions" checkbox that is required for each registration which clearly states the rules for your event such as no refunds, photos will be taken, etc.

Here are the terms and conditions we tend to use:

By checking the below box & completing your online registration, I acknowledge that I have read and I agree to abide by the Terms & Conditions listed below including giving us permission to take videos, photographs and use your image or likeness, at any time and for any legitimate purpose, agree that all sales are final and NO REFUNDS will be offered regardless of changes to venue, date, time, speakers, guest list, numbers of attendees, sponsors or other details. Furthermore, mistakes in event descriptions or text may occur and buyer is responsible for verifying any discrepancies or concerns prior to registration by contacting us via the contact us links or emails provided on event pages. You furthermore agree to contact us prior to attending the event or at most two (2) days after the event and clearly explain any issue. In extenuating circumstances and solely at our discretion, we may offer you a credit towards future events. If you do not accept our Terms & Conditions, do not register. Thank you for your cooperation.

Furthermore, you shall provide us with accurate, complete and current information during registration, and update the information provided to us if and as soon as such information should change. You also grant us permission to share your information with venue hosts and sponsors allowing them to share relevant information based on your interest.

You agree that you will not consume alcohol if you are not of the legal age, nor share alcohol with minors whether they are your guest or not. Furthermore, we reserve the right to refuse service to anyone at any time for any reason. We always reserve the right to ask you to leave an event at any time for any reason and may, at our discretion, refund you the cost of your ticket, minus any expenses or processing fee's.

The information provided by these workshops is intended for informational purposes only and accuracy is not guaranteed. The workshops are not intended to offer specific professional advice. Each business is unique, please consult with qualified professionals to discuss your situation.

If you have any questions or concerns please contact us by e-mail: info@piedmontave.com

Ticket registration

- ☐ Online ticketing
- ☐ Collect attendee data
- ☐ Don't ask too many questions
- ☐ Terms and Conditions included related to refunds, photos, etc.
- ☐ If you charge a fee, try to collect during registration
- ☐ Make sure a confirmation email goes out ASAP
- ☐ Optional: Pre-event survey (ask what they want and expect)

CHAPTER 4

SECURING VENUE AND EVENT SPONSORS

There are many different types of sponsors that can help by supporting your event. Some examples of sponsors include people or companies that donate trips, experiences, or art for a silent auction; media sponsors that help promote an event; restaurant sponsors that provide food; companies who provide sample products, services or assistance at the event; venue sponsors; local business sponsors; government sponsors and more.

Here is an example of how to ask for a venue sponsor:

Hi [NAME], You have a beautiful location and it would be an ideal venue for us to organize and host our business after work mixers, young professional happy hours, spirit and food tastings, or charity events.

Our company Piedmont Avenue Consulting / Professional Connector (www.ProfessionalConnector.com) has hosted and promoted 50+ events each year for the last 9 years at the most prestigious locations throughout the Bay Area including at Restaurants and Lounges (SOMAEats, Lucky Strike, Elévé, The Oxford, Build Pizzeria, Bling Tiger, Marriott Marquis View Lounge, King George Hotel, etc.) Country Clubs (Diablo, Oakhurst, Ruby Hill) and at other business and technology company locations (WeWork, Regus, General Assembly, Wix, Breather etc) and many more.

When working with venues, we typically select slower days of the week to allow us to bring in more people and not take away from any regular customer revenue or potential private event revenues. Venues may also invite loyal customers, guests, etc. to come to the networking event at no charge which helps with your overall customer loyalty program.

To get an idea. Below are some links to past events.

San Francisco Food Tech Mixer with Expert Panel
http://www.professionalconnector.com/event/san-francisco-foodtech-mixer

Young Professional Networking Mixer

http://www.professionalconnector.com/event/young-professionals-networking

East Bay Networking Mixer

http://www.professionalconnector.com/event/east-bay-business-networking

Vodka Tasting Event

http://www.professionalconnector.com/event/vodka-tasting-library-main/

If this is something of interest. We can discuss further to design some events to meet your needs.

Below are some sponsorship package examples:

PACKAGES

Bronze Tier includes: (If do 3+ events, 15% off for each event)

- 2 event tickets
- Space in the networking area for your marketing materials
- Opportunity to provide raffle item(s)
- Opportunity to provide handouts to participants
- Featured in our event promotion emails

- Included in the event Thank You email

Gold Tier includes benefits from Bronze Tier plus: (If do 3+ events, 15% off for each event)

- 4 event tickets
- Opportunity to include company information, logo and website in all advertisements of the events via email, social media, event website, and online event postings
- Opportunity to include company information and website link in follow-up email to participants
- Signage on the stage and/or networking area (if provided)
- Brief introduction of your company during the event to the group.

Platinum Tier includes benefits from Gold Tier plus: (If do 3+ events, 15% off for each event)

- 6 event tickets
- The company will be on the expert panel.
- The team member that will be on the panel will be featured as an expert. The company employee headshot and bio will be featured on the event page.
- Company logo and paragraph included on the event page, thank you email.

- Expert and Company feature in dedicated social media promotion shout out and featured in the email newsletter (35,000+ contacts)

Now that you have secured a space, created a strategy, set up your event webpage and have all of the materials in order, you can now use all of that to put together an event sponsorship proposal. The proposal will outline a deal between you and the sponsor. Typically, in exchange for food, samples, etc. for the event, you can offer free promotion of their products and/or services, tickets to the event or a table and/or area at the event for them to display their company.

CHAPTER 5

SPEAKERS AND
EXPERT PANELISTS

Are you looking to transform your event or conference? Having guest speakers, experts panel of founders, or hiring a professional keynote speaker will lead to greater attendance and publicity for your event. There are many ways to find speakers and experts to be a part of you event.

What Kind of Speaker Do You Need?

First, are you looking for a speaker to simply show up and give a talk and leave? Or do you want a speaker who becomes a part of the event and truly adds value to your entire conference? Some speakers will attend your cocktail receptions, be part of executive meetings, write blog articles or magazine articles prior to the event and/or post to promote the event and continue the learnings, etc.

Second, do you want a Motivational Speaker, Inspirational Speaker, Corporate Speaker, Marketing speaker or a Futurist who is talking about the latest trends.

Third, what type of event are you holding? Is this for a conference, corporate retreat, sales meeting, product launch, etc. and are you looking to educate, motivate, entertain, promote your brand, or a mixture.

Based on these three factors, you can then do Google searches and reach out directly to speakers if you are seeking local speakers or bring in out of town speakers on specific topics.

You can also look at similar events, conferences, etc. or ask others for referrals. Another approach, especially for the more celebrity speakers, is to contact speaker bureaus such as BigSpeak, Leading Authorities, Eagles Talent, etc.

Inviting Speakers or Experts via Linkedin:

We often use LinkedIn to invite founders and experts to be on our experts' panels or speakers at our events. We find that it is also a great way for the experts in a field to learn more about us and our company.

Here is an example of a LinkedIn message inviting someone to be a part of an event:

Hi [NAME], I am organizing a "Meet the Founders: FinTech Networking and Expert Panel" event on 8/22 from 6pm to 8pm at General Assembly SF and I would love to have you as part of our panel of experts. Let me know and I can tell you more.

OR the longer version:

Hi [NAME], I am organizing a FinTech event with an experts panel on 8/22 6pm to 8pm at General Assembly SF (225 bush St) and I would love to have you as part of our expert panel if you are available.

The panel is from 7:15pm to 7:45pm. It may run a little longer if attendees are having fun asking questions. There is no need to prepare; we keep it on a casual conversation format.

Here is more about the event
https://fintech-san-francisco.eventbrite.com

Let me know if you can make it and I will include you and your company on our event page.

How Much Does a Keynote Speaker Cost?

For determining how much a Keynote Speaker is paid, factors

include the duration and location of the event, career experience and significant life experiences of the speaker, how well known the speaker is, etc.

The amounts that keynote speakers charge can be a perception of quality. Speakers can also make adjustments to their prices when the audience is desirable to speak to or if they are already in the area. Depending on the speaker, there may often be a nonprofit rate or reduced rate for certain charity events. Typically, keynote speaker fee's can be broken down as follows:

- **Free** – This is usually a local speaker in the beginning of their career with little to no experience or speaking at the event is mutually beneficial for both parties involved. For instance, speakers can offer to speak at an event that will allow them to retain business from those within the audience due to the services they offer.

- **$500 – $1,500** – Small conferences and events try to obtain speakers at this cost. This is a humble number to obtain a keynote speaker. This range is for unestablished keynote speakers who are once again at the beginning of their career, but with slightly more experience. Typically, the event also promotes the speaker.

- **$1,500 – $5,000** – Keynote speaker fees in this range may be professional speakers with less experience speaking or achievements at this point in their career or life. The speaker adds value to the event and attracts more attendees.

- **$5,000 – $10,000** – This begins the range for professional keynote speakers. These are individuals who have given many speeches, have career accomplishments, and have established themselves in the keynote speaking industry. This is also when speakers are often speaking internationally. They likely have written a book(s).

- **$10,000 – $25,000** – These keynote speakers are distinguished speakers that have very successful accomplishments and experiences to draw from. An example would be a published author or founder of a successful company. It is not unusual that many large conferences pay this fee for their keynote speakers.

- **$25,000 – $50,000** – This range is for well-known individuals or celebrities with recognized names or titles, have extensive work and life experience to share, or individuals who have had a significant event impact their life. An example would be a famous professor from a university who discovered something.

- **$50,000 – $100,000** – This is the approximation for famous celebrity speakers. Organizations are more likely to invest in this price range for a keynote speaker if ticket sales are expected to exceed the price it would cost to retain a celebrity speaker.

- **$100,000+** – This is the ballpark for most famous politicians. This is the range if you are looking to have someone such as Barack Obama, Hilary Clinton, Donald Trump, etc. to speak at your event.

- **Travel Expenses** – Keep in mind that in addition to a speaker fee, there are usually travel related expenses. Often times, if the keynote speaker is not local, event or conference planners often offer to pay a flat fee or stipend for travel expenses such as flight + hotel. A fair amount for domestic travel is usually around $1500, which includes airfare, two nights in a hotel, ground transportation, meals, etc.

CHAPTER 6

PROMOTION TECHNIQUES: SOCIAL MEDIA

There are many places that you can choose to promote upcoming events you may have. On your website, it is always a good idea to feature your calendar as much as possible. Use the Internet to publicize your event and make it easier for your audience to gain information about it. Using the Internet is also convenient because you can make changes to the event, quickly notify people of upcoming events and interact with your audience.

Collaborating with others is a good way to relieve some of the burden of creating an entire event. Increase what the event has to offer and offset some of the workload by inviting others to present, provide something at your event, or help promote the event with you. This will help expand your client base as well as theirs.

Promotion: Once you've planned the event, the next step is to use a promotional mix of tools including the event page, email, social media, local online event calendars, strategic partners and media sponsors to successfully get the word out about your event.

Promote what you've got - An event can attract more business.

Collaborate with others - Get other businesses and charities involved.

Get the word out about your event by using sites that both empower event organizers to become more efficient and effective when bringing people together and allow you to promote and track attendance to see how many people are coming to your event. Improve the turnout of your event by communicating with your audience ahead of time.

Social Media for Event Promotion: Events are current and by listing them online you can increase your visibility by showing up today in search engine and social media results. There are endless ways to use social media to promote your events and keep in touch with attendees. To begin, you will need to create a marketing plan. The use of a marketing plan is to eliminate any confusion and to make sure that you always stay on the right track to reach the goal for your events.

Providing Updated Information About the Event: Keep people updated with the latest news regarding your event, last minute changes, or general information that includes addresses, time, date, parking information and other helpful tips related to the event.

Here are the top ways to promote your event:

LinkedIn: Millions of members have been increasingly utilizing the tool of LinkedIn to source and sign up to attend local or industry related events. It benefits event organizers, marketers and professionals alike. Can write a Linkedin post to promote the event.

Facebook: Create a Facebook page for your event. Include a brief topic description, information regarding any guest speakers, photos of the venue or important guest attendees, post event-related videos, and have a prominent "register now" button. By doing this on Facebook, you will also be able to reach a bigger audience, who may be potential customers.

Twitter: Post event links on Twitter informing followers about upcoming events. Come up with catchy hashtags (#) to create buzz as well as engage with your audience. Engage the Attendees of the event: This can be done through creating countdowns to the event, promotions, quick links to the official website, allowing attendees to share photos, posting statuses with special hashtags (#) and other elements. You can also create competitions or raffles with prizes or other types of compensation.

Instagram or Pinterest: Take photos before, during, and after your event and post them. You may also create an event countdown to raise awareness and engage potential customers. During the event, engage the audiences by encouraging them to take pictures and upload them with hashtags to Instagram or Pinterest.

Online registration-ticketing platforms: Utilizing online platforms, like Eventbrite and Meetup, allows for a more accessible event; leading to more attendees.

Team up with a Non-Profit: Your event will attract new target audiences while helping the community. By doing this, it will show that your business is interested in the success and well-being of the local community.

Create calendar invitations: Utilize your company email list when you're having an event, but do not overwhelm your customers with your invitations. Just simply send a reminder about the event as the date draws close. Keep it short and simple.

Online promotion: This includes social media, blogs, and other social networking platforms that specialize on events such as Meetup, LinkedIn and others. Throwing an event creates brand awareness, customer loyalty, reminds your audience that you exist and results in lead generation.

Email Newsletters: Email is a good place to start for the initial promotion of the event. Give your audience time to plan for the event by initiating contact around a month in advance. I like using platforms such as MailChimp, Constant Contact and Robly.

Using Media Sponsors: Another great way to promote your event is to get your media sponsors involved. Working with them to promote your event is a great way to reach a larger audience and increase the turnout. Your media sponsors can send emails to their audience and promote the event through their social media channels. Before your media sponsor promotes your event, provide them with a few guidelines to synchronize your marketing efforts with theirs in order to create a clear message.

YouTube videos: Create an enticing video that people will share. You can post the teaser of your next event, any videos from past events, or even testimonials from people to capture the interest of those you wish to attract. Do not forget to make sure that the video is high-quality with excellent images, a clear voice and a catchy introduction.

Share, Share and Share: Create custom social share buttons on your website to allow as many people as possible to share the event. Social share buttons consist of several sharing alternatives, including Like and Share on Facebook, LinkedIn, Twitter and other social media platforms. These methods have been proven as a great way to drive traffic back to your promotional page.

Follow Back/Socialize for Feedback: Promoting does not stop after the event has ended. Through social media you can follow up with the attendees, get feedback from them about what they liked best and least about the event and discover what people hope to see next time. In addition, you can use social media for pre-promotion for the next event.

Do not miss out on all the added value that can be created by utilizing the wonderful world of social media. We encourage you to be social and use all the capabilities of technology to promote your brand as well as events.

Local Calendar Sites: Websites for local newspapers and magazines are great places to list your events. There are also other platforms (www.FullCalendar.com) that will auto-post your events to the majority of local calendar sites.

Press Release Sites: To get the word out, attract media attention and have lots of back links to your website there are numerous free and paid press release submission sites such as:

- Cision
- PR Newswire (a Cision company)
- Business Wire
- Newswire
- Marketwired
- PRgloo

- PR Underground
- PRWeb

This is an example press release:

Silicon Valley International Invention Festival Exposition
Santa Clara Convention Center
5001 Great America Parkway Hall A
Santa Clara, CA 95054
https://sviif-expo-santa-clara.eventbrite.com

PRESS RELEASE

Tuesday, May 28th, 2019
FOR IMMEDIATE RELEASE
The World Intellectual Property Organization along with the Swiss Consulate General of San Francisco Hosts the Silicon Valley International Invention Festival Exposition - The Silicon Valley International Invention Festival Exposition will be held from Monday, June 24th to Wednesday, June 26th, 2019 from 10:00 AM to 5:00 PM. Join innovators, ground breakers, investors and visionaries at the Santa Clara Convention Center to broaden your network and learn from the most influential pioneers in leading industries.

During the Silicon Valley International Invention Festival Exposition there will be hundreds of new inventions presented by exhibitors coming from all over the world. You can't miss this opportunity to meet world-renowned inventors who will be presenting cutting-edge technology. Our wide variety of exhibitions span from lifestyle products which are used in everyday life, to ground-breaking innovations which push the boundaries of modern technology.

This one-of-a-kind opportunity will establish interactions directly with businessmen and representatives of international and local industrial companies and corporations. This innovative event will be located in the heart of high technology, another reason why innovators, funding professionals, entrepreneurs, engineers, investors, high ranking organizations, inventors' associations and the like should attend. Miss the Silicon Valley International Invention Festival Exposition and you might be missing the next big thing.

This event is not only perfect for individuals and companies who are curious about the latest inventions, it also is ideal for investors, venture capitalists, VC firms, angel investors, and startup

investors alike. We have personally invited professionals from such companies as Google Ventures, KKR & Co, Menlo

Ventures, Nexus Venture Partners, TriplePoint Capital, Highland Capital Partners, DCM Ventures, The Westly Group and more.

This event is supported by the World Intellectual Property Organization, the Swiss Consulate General of San Francisco, and the city and the University of Santa Clara in collaboration with the US Patent and Trademark Office. Silicon Valley International Invention Festival is hosted by the International Federation of Inventors Association (IFIA) and organized by PALEXPO SA who is also the organizer of the International Exhibition of Inventions Geneva.

Event information and complimentary registration https://sviif-expo-santa-clara.eventbrite.com

Please email info@piedmontave.com with any questions or inquiries.

Event Promotion Checklist:

- ☐ Have event calendar on company website? Is the calendar interactive? Is the calendar updated often?
- ☐ Event on industry related websites?
- ☐ Event on local event sites?
- ☐ Events show up in Google searches?

- ☐ Organization have a Meetup group? Sponsor a Meetup Group?
- ☐ Have an Eventbrite account?
- ☐ Post events on Facebook?
- ☐ Post events on Twitter?
- ☐ Event photos on company website?
- ☐ Slideshow or video from event on website or video channel?

CHAPTER 7

EMAIL MARKETING

Every email you send to potential or current customers can be considered email marketing. Email marketing is a quick, easy and low-cost option to reach your target markets. It could involve using emails to send advertisements, informational messages, and reminders, as well as to seek new business, request sales, refer other businesses and recommend action. If done correctly, email marketing can evoke and establish loyalty, reliability, trust and awareness. The most popular email marketing platforms for small businesses are MailChimp, Constant Contact and Robly.

Email Marketing for Events

Email marketing offers a variety of specialized uses that can be tailored to both your business and your customers. Email marketing can be a powerful marketing automation tool. Email

41

marketing can help energize your own online marketing strategy by:

- Increasing sales conversions: Prospects may require up to nine "touches" before making a buying decision. When you're communicating with new prospects, repetition isn't optional; It's mandatory. Sending emails is an inexpensive way to remind consumers you exist.

- Generating repeat sales: Obtaining new customers is much more expensive than selling to an existing one. Keeping in touch on a regular basis through email can generate repeat sales and improve customer loyalty.

- Up-selling and cross-selling your products: Email provides a great opportunity for you to help customers order "one more" product while they're in the mood to buy. It is easy to create a series of email messages that are timed to follow up with offers of related interest.

- Gaining feedback from your visitors: Email in particular provides your customers with a unique opportunity to give honest feedback. Now you're ready to adapt to what your market wants.

- Driving Web users to offline purchases: Email marketing is often a catalyst for Web users to purchase offline. More than half of users in one survey had made a purchase offline after receiving an email promotion.

Make it easy for customers to find you and see your business hours and other essentials.

The advantage of using email marketing is clear. The difficulty with email marketing is creating content that will be opened, read and clicked through. Think about your email inbox. What encourages you to open a message from a sender you are unaware of? What words draw you in? Inboxes are continuously cluttered and crowded with spam and other junk. The following tips are helpful for you to create an email marketing campaign that will generate a response.

- Be Concise: Make your emails short and to the point. No one wants to read through a 2,000-word email.
- Personalization: Address the person you are emailing by their name. People like to feel special. Write as if you are only emailing that one person.
- Offer Rewards: Offer a reward for reading the email. The reward doesn't have to be monetary. It can be a useful tip to help them in their life.
- Catchy Headline: The headline and subject line must attract attention. Otherwise readers will ignore it or delete it immediately. For events I like saying "You Are Invited..." or "Join 100+ Business Professionals at...".

- Draw On an Emotion: Create responsiveness by appealing to the reader's emotions and using sensory words

Using these tips does not guarantee a response. It is about experimenting to figure out what works best for your target audience and how they best respond to email marketing campaigns. It is an honor when people decide to become a part of your email marketing list. Be careful not to take advantage of this.

All that's left to do is press send and watch your business grow.

Everything You Need to Know About a Drip Campaign for Email Marketing

Newsletters are an effective way to reach and release your company's latest announcements. Many companies are using newsletters for email marketing, however there is a problem. Sending out a newsletter constantly can be very tedious and overwhelming for your subscribers. This is where drip campaigns can be very useful.

Drip Campaigns are known by other terms, drip marketing, automated email campaign, lifecycle emails, autoresponders and marketing automation. Others call it behavioral emails because these emails are modified based on the action the subscriber has performed (such as signing up for a service or making a purchase). All of these have the same concept. They are a set of emails that are sent out automatically on a pre-set time interval based on a specific timetable or user action. The purpose of doing drip campaigns is to give information to your audience at the right time. Drip Emails are producing 18 times more revenue than normal ones. According to research, drip emails increases click rates by 119%. Below are four major benefits of doing a drip campaign:

1. **Relevance:** Drip marketing delivers the appropriate information at the right time. If a person checks out a page or a product on your website, an automated campaign stimulates a thank you email for checking out the product.

2. **Creates Leads:** An important objective of drip marketing is to encourage early stage leads until they become more likely to make a purchase or accept a service.

3. **Reminders:** You are able to remind subscribers at periodic intervals about what you have to offer, which keeps you on their minds constantly.

4. **Work Smarter:** Since drip marketing is automated, it saves a lot of time and helps to nurture your leads for

you, so you can focus on closing deals instead of making marketing sales pitches.

What are you waiting for? To implement a drip campaign, you can set it up yourself by using the services of a platform like Constant Contact, Mailchimp or Robly. Use a drip campaign to help save time and earn your business money through email marketing.

Add Registrants to Customer Loyalty Program:

- ☐ Email marketing – Constant Contact, Robly, MailChimp
- ☐ Make sure to announce any major changes that are made to the event page once it's published.

CHAPTER 8

EVENT TIMELINE

When planning an event, depending on the site of the event (conferences, company sales retreats, festivals, etc.) you may need to plan years ahead as big venues are booked far out in advance. If your event is local or you have flexibility this is more of the standard event timeline.

60+ days:

Strategy and Secure space (Budget, Staffing, Create Website / Ticketing, Contact Media, Obtain Sponsors, etc.)

45 days:

Email Marketing and Social Media Marketing (Facebook, Twitter, Linkedin, meetup groups, etc.) Send out emails promoting the event. The best days to send out emails as well as to post on social media, (Facebook, Twitter, and LinkedIn) meetup groups, or other sites are Tuesday, Wednesday, and Thursday.

15 days:

Send reminder emails and repost/update Social Media. Confirm with staff and volunteers. Walkthrough of the space. Announce any new sponsors or raffle prizes that are consistent with the theme of event. Reconfirm with staff and volunteers, and do a walkthrough of the space.

Week of event:

Send email to specific groups (VIP's, Media, etc.) of people that you really want to come to your event.

Day before event:

Send reminder emails to your entire email list to reach everyone who is registered.

- Use first name
- Reconfirm with registration

- Describe the check-in process, where to park, what to bring, etc. Reiterate the event details, theme, speakers, etc. and tell people the event is going to be a success and that lots of people have already registered.

CHAPTER 9

DAY OF EVENT

Now that you have put in all the work for the pre-event strategies, the day of the event has finally come.

Check In Process:

Print out a list of your attendees for the check-in process before the event starts. Check people in and confirm their information (name, email address, phone number, etc.). Collecting information from the event attendees is crucial for success. You want to be able to contact each and every person that attends. Be prepared to collect walk-in's information for those that show up and have not registered. Many attendees will bring their business cards to hand out at the event. You can collect these business cards for a raffle or drawing. Expect that not all of those who registered will show up for the event. Remember for a public free event, you can you can expect that 40%-60% of RSVPs will show up. For paid public events, 85% of RSVPs typically show up. Factors such as the theme of the event, reminder emails, targeted reminder phone calls to key people, great Keynote Speaker, influencers posting to social media about attending the event, the weather being not too hot and no too cold, no major sporting event, etc. can all increase or decrease the attendance.

Although the preparation for the event is complete, the day of an event can be pretty hectic.

Volunteers: It may be beneficial to have a few volunteers to help with setting up the event, greeting people and assisting you in making sure the event runs smoothly.

Thank your sponsors and attendees: Remember to take the time out at the event to thank the sponsors for supporting the event. You also want to thank the attendees for showing up. One way you can do this is by providing them with a complimentary discount or gift bag as a token of your appreciation. Check with your sponsors to see if they have something that can be donated for the gift bags to add value for the attendees.

Encourage use of social media: Encourage event attendees to tweet, post on Instagram, check-in on Facebook and share their experience online. Create a unique, catchy hashtag (#) for social media users to incorporate into their postings.

Day of Event:

☐ Print out attendee list, check people in and confirm info. Be prepared to collect walk-in's info. Collect business cards for raffle.

Activities at the Event:

☐ Fundraising
☐ Collect money at Event
☐ Selling Products at the Event
☐ Thank Sponsors
☐ Event to Next Event

CHAPTER 10

POST-EVENT FOLLOW-UP PROCEDURES

The event is over, however your job is not. If you want to maximize the effort you put into the event, following up is a key aspect.

Days Following the Event

Send out a follow up email to all REGISTERED attendees, not just people who actually attended to thank them for attending. "We had a great turnout and a great event, thanks to our sponsors and volunteers, etc." Be sure to address the guest by first name in the email (do this easily by using a platform such as Constant Contact or Mailchimp).

If pictures were taken at the event, include at least one photo from the event in the email and let people know more pictures are coming soon.

Provide an incentive to participate in a survey (ask what they liked about the event or what they would change about it). 'Thank you in advance for taking time to share your event experience with us'.

Ask people to post, tweet and comment about their experience.

Provide them with sample content. If you gave a presentation, offer to email a copy of the presentation.

Emphasize a call to action. Why did you have the event? What did you want to get out of having the event?

If you have another event coming up - promote it!

1-2 days following the event:

- ☐ Send email to all REGISTERED attendees (not just people who actually attended) to thank them for attending a successful event.

- ☐ Link to pictures from the (have them on your website or social media)
- ☐ Provide an incentive to participate in a survey
- ☐ Ask people to post, tweet, comment about their experience.
- ☐ If you gave a presentation, link to copy of the presentation in the thank you email.
- ☐ Emphasize a call to action: Why did you have the event?
- ☐ If you have another event coming up - mention it.

CHAPTER 11

EVENT PLATFORMS: MEETUP AND EVENTBRITE

Events are a fun option to create more awareness surrounding your company, while simultaneously allowing you to build relationships with likeminded individuals. The following are sites that are helpful to plan and promote events.

Meetup for Business

Meetup.com is a useful site for people to promote their local business. The goal is to "revitalize local community and help people around the world self-organize." Meetup helps people to meet offline and save time and costs by inviting others to attend events. Meetup has over 25+ million members and is the world's largest network for local groups. It has around 9 million visitors every month, in 45,000 cities across 179 countries and 600,000+ monthly meetups on every topic. People use Meetup to find individuals with the same interests, to attend events and to promote their business. This is an easy and effective way for individuals to connect and network with one another.

Here are five helpful tips to get you started on Meetup

Create a Meetup Account:

Pick a topic related to your business or an interest your target audience has. Create a detailed description of what you do, the kinds of members who would be interested and who would be a good fit to join your group. When creating a group, choose a narrow topic that is something unique to distinguish yourself from other similar groups in your area.

Organize regular meetups:

As soon as you have created a group on Meetup, start organizing regular meetups such as workshops, seminars, or networking events sponsored by your business. Make sure your Meetup group has some members before organizing your first meetup.

Connect your Facebook to Meetup:

Connecting your Facebook to Meetup is an easier way to promote what you have been organizing on your Meetup group. Your friends on Facebook will see what you are up to and vice versa.

Message your members:

Once you gain some members, start messaging them about the upcoming events you are planning. Getting in touch with your members is a great way to keep them interested and active in your group.

Don't make it all about you and your business:

Your guests are not planning on attending your event to hear all about what you do or what your business offers (even if you're the one who organized the meetup). They are interested in meeting individuals who share the same interest and bond over current issues of common interest. Give them a chance to speak and share thoughts, this will show that you genuinely care about them.

Being an organizer gives you the power of authority and allows you to demonstrate your capabilities as a business person. The purpose of organizing events is for your members to get to know you in person. People are more likely to do business with a person they like and respect. I organize networking meetups and have over 25 different targeted meetup groups. If you want to learn more about how to effectively promote events and maximize the use of Meetup, check out my events website Professional Connector (www.ProfessionalConnector.com). You can come as my guest to one of my events to meet me and other individuals who share the same interests that you do. Send me an email at David@PiedmontAve.com

Eventbrite for Business

With Eventbrite's professional and customizable tools, planning an event is made easy. Not only can you custom your event, you can also access your event registration page anywhere using their easy to use mobile application. Their services also give you the option to cross-promote your event to any of your social media accounts. You create a customized event registration page. Eventbrite lets you customize your event's registration form so you can decide how much information you want to collect from your attendees.

Need help spreading the word about your event? Eventbrite makes getting the word out easy with personalized emails and adding the events to search engines. Once your event is live on Eventbrite, you are given the option to send out emails to registered attendees. After you have started promoting the event you can also track your attendance to see how many people are coming to your event, the ticket and registration sales and ramp up your marketing activity as needed.

Not only does Eventbrite help you plan and promote your event, it also helps manage event entry with their Entry Manager app to check people in and scan barcoded tickets through your phone. If that isn't for you, you can print out a guest list to check people in. Eventbrite reaches a huge audience, makes life easier and helps to gain traffic to your website.

Eventbrite is an all in one tool with everything you need to sell tickets and manage registrations for any kind of event of any size. This is a great option because it is a free and easy online tool that helps you create, find and attend events. IF your event is paid, Eventbrite does take a percentage.

With Eventbrite anyone can be a great event organizer and empowers event organizers to become more efficient and effective when bringing people together. People everywhere are searching Eventbrite to discover great events that matter to them.

CHAPTER 12

FIVE COMMON
EVENT MISTAKES

Mistake #1: Overlooking Competing Events

When picking a date for an event, do not dismiss overlapping events. You're going to put so much effort into getting people's attention regardless. Don't let the reason people miss your event be because you did not realize that DreamForce was the same time. At the same time we have also had happy hours or expert panel events which have a related to a nearby big event theme (not competing with the other event or conference), which attracts people to our event.

Mistake #2: Not Confirming With Your Sponsors, Venue, & Speakers

There are a lot of moving pieces when planning an event. It can easily get confusing managing different groups of people, especially if they are coming at different times. The best approach is to have a written agreement with your vendors so that they know where, when, and what they will be accountable for. A few days before the event, check back in and remind them of their responsibilities. Always touch base with the venue at least two times as your event is getting closer. Employees leave or change positions, calendars get mixed up, and lots of things happen as your event date arrives. Staying in contact with the venue is critical.

Mistake #3: Not having a Plan B

Things happen, people and technology are not always reliable. Remain resilient if a vendor cancels last minute, an expert speaker no shows, the computer crashes, or you forget the presentation. You may have a clear idea of exactly how an event will go, but the truth is that it is never what you expect. Sometimes that's for better or worse. By coming into an event over-prepared, you will be able to relax and roll with the punches. "Hope for the best, plan for the worst."

Mistake #4: Not Gathering ALL the guest information

You're going to want to remember who showed up to your event. Gathering business cards at check-in is a great way to know who is there and what they do. Also, if someone didn't register before the event, you now have their information to add to your network.

Mistake #5: Not Following up AFTER the event

You've held a successful event; people enjoyed their time and you made your impact. Now what? It is essential that you thank the people that not only attended the event AND also those that signed up, yet did not attend. Whether they showed up or not, they have become a part of your network, and showing people gratitude is one of the fundamentals to building new relationships. Remember a big part of the reason you did the event is for the connections, leads, and opportunities; So follow up! This is the biggest reason to host events - generate new opportunities by follow up.

CHAPTER 13

NETWORKING EVENTS DO'S AND DON'TS

Networking is an art, and there's a way to master it. The saying, "It's all about who you know" holds true to this day. Expand your network to create long lasting relationships to help you thrive in the business world. If you are someone who is looking to improve your networking skills, this page is the place for you. These tips are designed to help you succeed at networking both online and at events. Over the years, I have gathered some tips and tricks I've learned to help you excel at networking.

Networking events are great places to meet new people and find potential connections. Going to events is an excellent way to meet new people who you can also work with. The most common question we receive regarding events is "What should I bring?" Here is a list of how to be successful at networking events:

- Bring your business card – enough to hand out
- Dress to impress – you never know who you'll meet
- Have a goal – ask yourself "Why am I going?"
- Bring a positive attitude – make a good first impression
- Bring your social skills – remember what you are there to do

Networking Do's

While networking events are great to go to, there is a method to the madness. When hosting networking events, we always get the question of "What should I do?" or "What do I do now?" Here are the do's and don'ts when it comes to networking etiquette.

- Discuss commonalities
- Be a listener
- Ask questions
- Give out your business cards when appropriate
- Connect with people on LinkedIn
- Follow up within 72 hours
- Focus on quality, not quantity

Bring Business Cards:

Bring your business card to hand out to the people you connect with. This is important because the person you connect with will have all of your contact information and the necessary means to get ahold of you.

Ask Yourself Why You're Going:

What is the purpose of you attending this event? What are you trying to get out of it? Establish your purpose before you go, and try to fulfill your goal during and after the event.

Discuss Commonalities:

Discussing commonalities is important for the reason of seeing if it makes sense for the both of you to connect. It is possible that two people can be in completely different fields of work, but have a commonality that connects them.

Be A Listener:

First and foremost, listen to others. No one likes people who only talk about themselves without giving the other person a chance to talk. Listen to what others have to say and engage in healthy conversation. People like to talk about themselves.

Ask Questions:

This goes along with being a listener. Ask questions about people's lives and maybe you'll both know the same person. If you don't ask someone questions about themselves, they might think you are not interested or don't care.

Follow up Within 72 Hours:

You hand out your business card to people you like for a reason. Utilize their contact info and reach out with an email or a request to connect on Linkedin. Sending a simple message saying "It was nice to meet you at the networking event" goes a long way.

Focus on Quality, not Quantity:

At networking events, you are probably not going to meet everyone there. With that said you are probably not going to like everyone you meet. Focus on connecting with one good person rather than trying to meet everyone at the event.

Networking Don'ts

As we've seen some great actions that help you succeed at networking events, we've also seen what not to do when networking. Here are some of the big does and don'ts when trying to expand your network.

Don'ts:

- Don't be a card dealer
- Do not be a "product pusher"
- Don't be a stalker
- Don't ask for a job
- Don't go with friends (or at least don't spend all your time with them)
- Don't discuss inappropriate topics
- Don't brag

Don't be a Card Dealer:

The reason for bringing business cards is to hand them out to a select few. You don't want to pass them out like candy. The goal of the night should not be for everyone at the event to have your business card, only the people you want to connect with.

Don't be a 'Product Pusher':

A product pusher is someone who tries to sell their product to the guests at the event. The event is not your time to sell your product or service. However, it is an opportunity for you to partner with someone who is interested in helping you sell or investing in it.

Don't ask for a job:

It is a myth that people go to networking events to hand out jobs. If you are in search of a job, connect with someone who could potentially put you in a position to help you find one. Asking for a job after meeting someone 30 minutes prior is not the time.

Don't go with friends:

Everyone has a different opinion on this idea. I have noticed that friends usually tend to stick together rather than branch out to meet new people. Move out of your comfort zone and try to attend an event alone (or when with friends separate for a while at the event), you never know who you might meet!

Don't discuss inappropriate topics:

Networking events are the time to meet new people and find new connections. It is not a time or place to discuss controversial topics or engage in a discussion that could lead to an argument.

Don't brag:

Finally, don't brag about yourself. There is a fine line between talking about yourself versus bragging about yourself. If you have an accomplishment that you are proud of, find an appropriate time to bring it up. Maybe your accomplishment can inspire or help someone else fulfill their goals.

While there are some tips and tricks to networking, it isn't magic. Have fun, be yourself and meet new people. We hope these do's and don'ts will help you in your networking events to come.

CHAPTER 14

RESOURCES

Piedmont Avenue Consulting, Inc. and Professional Connector are a registered partners with numerous companies whose products and solutions we use to streamline our clients business processes and promote our events. Below are some of the products and resources we use and recommend:

Robly

Robly is a leading innovator in Small Business Marketing Automation. Robly invented OpenGen and the Social Automation technology IntelliPost. Robly's breakthrough OpenGen technology starts with a regular email campaign send. OpenGen will then re-send your campaign 1 to 10 days later, with a different subject line of your choosing, only to those subscribers who didn't open the first campaign. Instead of sending your email campaign all at once, patent-pending Robly A.I. sends each email one at a time, at the exact moment your subscriber is most likely to check their inbox.

vCita

vCita is an appointment scheduler and customer relationship management platform which enables you to capture more new clients and provide better service to your existing clients. vCita provides lead generation, online scheduling, and invoicing for small businesses all in one easy to use resource. Visit www.bitly.com/vcita-piedmontave

Cogsworth

Cogsworth is a smart schedule management software designed to help businesses effectively manage their appointments and bookings.

WP Engine

WP Engine is a Hosted service provider, specifically tailored to WordPress websites and apps. Visit bit.ly/PACwpengine

Freshbooks

FreshBooks is a cloud-based accounting software service designed for owners of the types of small client-service businesses that send invoices to clients and get paid for their time and expertise. Visit Freshbooks.com

ZipRecruiter

ZipRecruiter is an online job distribution and job board service. The web-based platform aggregates applications from job boards and provides tools for applicants tacking and screening. Visit bit.ly/pac-ziprecruiter

Gusto

Gusto is reimagining payroll, benefits, and HR for modern companies. Gusto's mission is to create a world where work empowers a better life. By making the most complicated business tasks simple and personal, Gusto serves over 40,000 companies nationwide. Use link http://shrsl.com/jgvy for 1st month Free

Eventbrite

Eventbrite is a global marketplace for live experiences that allows people to find and create events in 190 countries. The platform allows event organizers to plan, promote, and sell tickets to events (event management) and publish them across Facebook, Twitter and other social-networking tools directly from the site's interface. It also enables attendees to find and purchase tickets to these experiences. Visit http://www.eventbrite.com/r/walnutcreekevents

Basecamp

Basecamp is more than just a project management tool — it's an elevated way to work. ... They're more productive and better organized. ... Create to-do lists for all the work you need to do, assign tasks, and set due dates. Basecamp puts everything you need to get work done in one place. It's the calm, organized way to manage projects, work with clients,
Visit http://bit.ly/basecampprojects

Bitly

Bitly is a link management platform. Bitly shortens 600 million links per month, for use in social networking, SMS, and email. Visit bit.ly/R5aB9v

Instapage

Instapage allows you to get more from your digital advertising spend. Own your post-click experience and maximize your conversion rates with Instapage, the most powerful landing page platform for marketing teams and agencies.

Join Our Partner Program:

Piedmont Avenue Consulting, Inc. and Professional Connector Partnership Program is perfect for established and new companies who want more brand awareness. We will use your product and feature you product on our website, events, and more. If you are interested in being part of our partner program, contact us at info@piedmontave.com for more information.